WONDERAMA

The Bob McAllister Years

by

Jay Jennings

Retro Image Publishing

Los Angeles, California

Wonderama: The Bob McAllister Years
Copyright © 2014 by Jay Jennings

ISBN 9781633181199

Published by Retro Image Publishing
Los Angeles, California
www.retroimagepublishing.blogspot.com

Printed in the United States of America

This book is dedicated to the late, great, Bob McAllister, a warm and kind-hearted soul who made Sunday mornings in the 1960s and 70s a fun time for us kids. He truly cared about kids and never spoke down to them. He entertained us with his funny skits, amazing magic, and catchy songs, all of which reminded us that "Kids Are People Too."

Contents

Acknowledgments

I would like to thank the following people whose contributions helped make this book possible: Susan Abbott, Molly McAllister, Robin C. Voth, Greg Voth, Don Spielvogel, Kevin Butler, and Billy Ingram of tvparty.com.

Except for the first chapter, all the photographs in this book are courtesy of Bob McAllister's family and Bob's assistant, Don Spielvogel.

Introduction

If you were a young child in the late 1960s or late 1970s, Wonderama is one of those surreal childhood memories that you're not sure actually existed or if you dreamed it. You have vague memories of a Sunday morning TV show and it's laid back, fun-loving host who sang catchy songs like "Exercise", introduced magicians and famous celebrities, and had kids in the audience play really cool games like "Snake Cans." In essence, your childhood went by so fast and today you're an adult with a family and kids of your own, so trying to recall the details of this unique kids show is riddled with flashing mental images of kids dancing to Elton John's "Crocodile Rock" and wearing Lender's Bagels necklaces.

The good news is you weren't dreaming. Wonderama was as real as the breakfast cereal you ate every morning while searching for the free prize at the bottom of the cereal box. In fact, Wonderama was an institution on Sunday morning television from 1955 to 1977 and little eyes were always glued to the TV set whenever it came on. One could even say that Wonderama's magnetic appeal to children was simply magical.

In the show's 22 year history, five capable hosts, all with their own schtick and sense of humor, left their indelible mark during the course of their hosting duties, but the one that seems to have left the most permanent impression was the fifth and final host, a ventriloquist-magician from Virginia who began hosting local children's shows in 1954 whose name was Bob McAllister.

During his tenure on Wonderama, Bob was the cool uncle that you wished was a part of your family. His charm and warmth toward the kids in the audience was genuine. He was real and down-to-earth and he never talked down to the children. He was interested in what they had to say, like a younger, more hipper, Art Linklater. That was a big part of the show's appeal and why the waiting list for tickets was seven years.

Not only did Wonderama feature popular games, contests, segments, and songs, but it was also the "Tonight Show" for kids, as a literal "Who's Who" of the entertainment world appeared on the show, and some more than once. Film and television stars, magicians, singers, bands, performers, and professional athletes all appeared on Bob's show, demonstrating their craft and giving advice to the young audience. Some of the more memorable guests included Muhammad Ali and Joe Frazier playing marbles before their big fight; Marty Allen and Bob wrestling; Billy Preston rocking the house with a rousing version of "Will It Go Round In Circles"; Paul Lynde sitting with the kids in the audience; Mel Blanc demonstrating all his famous cartoon voices.

Bob's version of Wonderama ran from 1967-77 with the last show being on Christmas Day. It's been said that since Wonderama went off the air, there has been a large void in children's programming. Truer words were never spoken. Its seems that mindless and/or violent cartoons have filled the space left by Wonderama and that TV stations simply have no interest in resurrecting similar type shows. It's too bad that children of the 1980s, 90s, and 2000s never got to experience the magic of Wonderama. What is even sadder is that no episodes of Wonderama were saved for future generations, as all the original tapes were either taped over or thrown in the East River by WNEW to make room in their vaults.

After many years of research, along with the invaluable contributions of Bob McAllister's family, I have put together this book about Wonderama, which features 200 never-before-published photographs. Now you can relive all your favorite segments, songs, games, contests, and guests that made Bob McAllister's Wonderama so memorable. "Wackadoo, wackadoo, wackadoo!"

— Jay Jennings

CHAPTER 1

The First Hosts

Wonderama made its debut on September 25, 1955 on WABD-TV (later WNEW) Channel 5 in New York City with the engaging Sandy Becker as host. Becker, with his comic voices and various hand puppets had already made a name for himself by hosting a popular morning and afternoon show earlier that year. Wonderama ran for six hours every Sunday from 12 p.m. to 6 p.m., as Becker entertained his young viewers with games, craft-making, puppetry, and skits, as well as, interviews with performers. Becker's co-host, Pat Meikle, would draw pictures and perform home-cooking lessons. Al Hodge ("Captain Video") and Melbourne Christopher would perform magic tricks and introduce old movie serials. Artist Jon Gnagy also had a compelling segment called "Learn to Draw." The intention behind Becker's variety of entertainment was to teach lessons and skills that would help children become better people. (Photo courtesy of Baby Boomer eMuseum).

Herb Sheldon replaced Becker as host of Wonderama on September 16, 1956, moving the show to Sunday mornings. Becker decided to quit after one year since he was hosting 11 programs and broadcasting six days a week. Sheldon had experience hosting children's shows on WNBT-TV (later WNBC) in New York City and he hosted Wonderama all by himself. The only other performers on the show were two puppets, Egbert the Bookworm and Ummley the Steam Shovel. Sheldon had a gentle, soft-spoken demeanor, talking to the kids at home in a fun and intelligent way, encouraging them to play games, telling charming stories, creating crafts, giving hobby tips, and instilling good values. Unfortunately, Sheldon had a past history of working for other stations in the city even though he was under contract, which would later prove to be his undoing with WABD-TV. While hosting Wonderama, Sheldon also took on the hosting duties of multiple children's shows, a dance show, and a late night movie show (all non-WABD programs), which left station management no choice but to terminate his contract on August 8, 1958. (Photo courtesy of tvparty.com)

On August 10, 1958, Bill Britten, an actor and puppeteer, became Wonderama's third host. Britten had studied to be a professional clown. This was the first version of Wonderama to be taped in front of a live studio audience. He initially hosted the show as "Three Gun Willie the Kid", but the character proved to be unpopular and was dropped. Doris Faye served as co-host. A variety of games, songs, stories, and skits made up the majority of the program. On September 7, 1958, WABD-TV became Metromedia WNEW-TV. Britten didn't stick around for very long, as he left the show at the end of December 1958 to become New York's world famous "Bozo the Clown" which he portrayed on WPIX-TV until 1964. (Photo courtesy of tvparty.com).

Wonderama's next host would also become one of its most popular. 1959 ushered in the era of Sonny Fox, who previously hosted children's travelogue shows. Fox was wildly popular with the kids, as he took Wonderama into a more educational direction, introducing new segments such as spelling bees, dance lessons, and Shakespeare dramatizations, not to mention, trips to places and events of interest to the kids. Fox had a special rapport with children that allowed him to entertain and teach them without appearing boring or patronizing. Suave, congenial, and dryly witty, Fox balanced effortlessly between the serious and slapstick, turning Wonderama's Sunday marathon of four hours into a weekly academy at which anything could happen and often did. Around the same time, Fox hosted two other game shows for kids, "Just For Fun" and "On Your Mark". He would end up hosting Wonderama for almost nine years until August 6, 1967, when he left to host a talk show for women called "The New Yorkers.". One week later, on August 13, 1967, Wonderama would get its fifth and final host, a 13-year veteran of hosting children's shows in Norfolk, Virginia and Baltimore, Maryland. His name was Bob McAllister. (Photo courtesy of tvparty.com).

CHAPTER 2

Meet Bob McAllister

Bob McAllister hosted eight different children's TV shows between 1954-78, talking to kids and engaging them in all sorts of games and fun activities. Bob once said that all he ever wanted to do was talk to children because he related to them. Kids are important and have things to say and Bob wanted to give them a platform to speak their mind and have fun at the same time. This is why his version of Wonderama was so different from the four previous ones, and why Bob, himself, was a unique host.

Bob McAllister was born in Philadelphia, Pennsylvania on June 2, 1935 and raised in upstate New York and later in Virginia. Bob had been interested in magic and ventriloquism from a very early age. He appeared at many local parties and charity events to entertain children and sick people. Every day, he practiced illusions and ventriloquism. When Bob received at least a B in all his classes at Granby High, his mother bought him his first vent figure (ventriloquist dummy) which he named "Chauncey."

In 1953, Bob's parents took him to New York City. During their trip, Bob snuck out of the hotel room and went with his vent figure Chauncey to the sidewalk studios of "The Today Show" on West 49th Street. Bob had his puppet dressed up like the show's first host, Dave Garroway, holding a sign against the glass window of the studio that read, "Peace." Garroway then invited Bob to come into the studio to do his act on live television.

Bob did so well on "The Today Show" that Garroway got him an audition for CBS' "Ted Mack and his Original Amateur Hour." Bob appeared on the show in 1953 as both a magician and ventriloquist and even though he came in 2nd place, the enthusiastic audience was very impressed with Bob's performance.

In 1954, after a brief stint in college and working at radio station WRVA in Richmond, Virginia, Bob went to work at WVEC-TV Channel 15 in Norfolk, where his duties included several jobs, including programming director.

Later in the year when WVEC-TV needed a children's TV program for their weekday morning schedule, they hired Bob to host "Ranch House Tales", introducing old cowboy movies.

    In 1956, Bob joined joined CBS affiliate, WTAR-TV Channel 3 in Norfolk, hosting "The Little Rascals Clubhouse" which later became "The Bob and Chauncey Show." Famous kiddie show hosts like Captain Kangaroo appeared on the show, which also featured Bob's original puppets and other goofy characters.

Also in 1956, Bob hosted "The Bozo Show" on WTAR-TV and made public appearances all over Norfolk, Virginia, as Bozo the Clown.

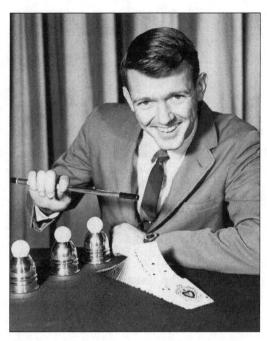

In 1963, Bob moved to WJZ-TV Channel 13 in Baltimore, Maryland, where he served as assistant puppeteer and magician every weekday morning on "The Lorenzo Show" (played by actor Jerry Wheeler).

Around the same time, Bob started hosting "The Bob & Chauncey Show" on Saturday mornings on WJZ-TV.

In 1964, Bob replaced "The Lorenzo Show" and started hosting "The Bob McAllister Show" every weekday morning, making balloon animals, performing comedy skits, magic tricks, and songs. The show also featured Bob's main vent figure, Chauncey, as well as, a cast of puppets like Seymour Snake (who gave the daily weather forecast), Sylvester Rivets the Robot, and the Nudnicks (who were made from toilet plungers).

The cast of characters on the show (all played by Bob) were the evil Silas Sinister, Thurmin the Country Bumpkin, Zip Code the Hippy, Professor Fingleheimer, Charlie Chin, a London Bobby, a French Chef, and the clown twins, Willy Winkie and Billy Blinkie.

By far, the most popular character on Bob's show was the bumbling superhero, Mike Fury, who wore a cape and goggles and would sing: "Mike Fury is a goody!" Fury would constantly foil the evil Silas Sinister and his dastardly plans.

During the three years he hosted his popular WJZ-TV show, Bob had been writing and sending audition tapes to New York stations in hopes of landing a major gig.

In 1967, Bob's persistence paid off, as his Baltimore show and talents came to the attention of the executives at WNEW-TV Channel 5 in New York City who were looking for a children's TV host to succeed Sonny Fox, who was leaving the popular kids show, "Wonderama." Bob went to the Big Apple to audition for it. Needless to say, he got the job and the rest, as they say, is history.

CHAPTER 3

TV Tapings

Bob McAllister began hosting Wonderama on WNEW-TV Channel 5 in New York on August 13, 1967. The show aired Sunday mornings from 7:30 a.m. to 11:00 a.m. (later from 8 a.m. to 11 a.m.).

Besides New York, the show ran nationwide in six other major markets in which Metromedia owned television stations. Those stations were KTTV Los Angeles, WXIX Cincinnati, WTCN Minneapolis/St. Paul, KMBC Kansas City, WCVB Boston, and WTTG Washington D.C.

The show consisted of eight-hour tape days which was staged at WNEW/Metromedia television studios at 205 East 67th Street, on the fifth floor in Studio 5.

Wonderama's TV tapings were done on Wednesdays and then later moved to Thursdays between 1:00 p.m. and 9:00 p.m. and all the parents and kids didn't start to line-up outside the studio until after the talk show "Midday Live" went off the air at noon.

The day's taping was divided into 13 segments which enabled the six other Metromedia stations running Wonderama in their cities to drop in their own commercials and give stagehands a chance to switch props and allow the kids in the audience to use the bathroom.

The seating capacity always varied, depending on how large the audience was. Bob's early Wonderama shows had five rows of kids, while in the show's later years, there were as many 10 rows of kids.

The parents who wanted to stay and keep an eye on their kids were kept in a lecture room on the 6th floor called Kluge Hall which had easy chairs and soft drinks, and a couple of big monitors to watch the taping.

Wonderama's segments were all planned and outlined by Bob and his staff earlier in the week. When it was time to tape the show, Bob would then engage his studio audience (between 100 to 175 kids), age 7 to 14, with magic tricks, comedy skits, songs, games and contests, and several breaks to run old cartoons.

When Bob first took over Wonderama in 1967, the show featured occasional celebrity guests like Sally Field ("The Flying Nun") or the cast of "What's My Line?", as well as, musical performances by Jefferson Airplane or Vanilla Fudge(!), but from 1970-77, Wonderama would welcome famous actors, singers, musicians, comedians, athletes, magicians, and experts in various fields on every single show, thus Wonderama became known as "The Tonight Show" for kids.

Before every TV taping, Bob would come out and remind the kids to be polite and to respect all the guests. But most importantly, he reminded them that not everyone will win a special prize but that everyone would be going home with a bag of goodies, much to their screaming delight.

All the kids in the studio audience also received a Lender's Bagels necklace with their name hand-painted on the front that they would proudly wear throughout the whole show. At every taping, Lender's would send in a couple of artists who would hand paint each kid's name on a bagel necklace before the show began. Once in a while, a couple of kids would get hungry during the show and try to eat their bagel necklace.

During the show's lunch break, all the kids were treated to Good Humor Ice Cream and RC Cola.

Bob's main goal on Wonderama was to inform and entertain and sometimes educate. Bob didn't think it was the job of a children's TV show host to be an educator. That job was for parents and school teachers.

During Bob's 10+ years as host, Wonderama was seen by six to 10-million viewers every Sunday morning, making Bob the king of Sunday morning television, as the show attracted more than half of the Sunday morning audience, according to Nielsen ratings. Bob's office received 3,000 requests a week for the limited studio seats that were available.

Producers of Wonderama over the years included Art Stark (former producer of Johnny Carson's "Tonight Show"), Artie Forrest (who later directed "The Rosie O'Donnell Show"), the late Dennis Marks (who worked on the original game show "Concentration"), and the late comedian David Brenner.

Chet Lishawa was the director of Wonderama who later became a director at Fox News, while Associate Producer Jan Bridge secured all the music. Bob's assistant and close friend, Don Spielvogel, helped make sure that each show went smoothly, even entertaining the kids in the audience during each break.

CHAPTER 4

Segments & Games

Bob McAllister's Wonderama, for the most part, had the same format every week. The three hour show consisted of a familiar set of songs that Bob would sing, as well as, an array of entertaining segments and fun games, plus two or three special guests or performers.

Since the show basically kept to this formula, the kids in the audience and the millions watching at home, not only knew what games, contests, songs, and segments to expect, but they anxiously looked forward to it.

Wonderama had two different openings. The first one had Bob bursting through a large banner that read, "Wonderama", as he would motion for you to join him. The second opening had Bob declaring, "All these kids are here because this is Wonderama!" The kids would scream and cheer when Bob made his entrance.

At the beginning of each show, Bob would greet the kids by singing, "Hello, Hello", in which he would welcome all the kids and tell them how glad he was to see them.

Bob would then briefly go over what games and segments were planned for the day, followed by who the guests were going to be.

Next, Bob would go into the audience and sing, "Good News", in which he would ask the kids if they had any good news for him. During the song, different kids would reply into Bob's microphone with, "I have a new dog", or "my mom's having a baby", or "I'm on Wonderama!"

Sometimes if one of Bob's guests was already sitting in the audience, he would sit down next to them for an impromptu interview and if they were funny (like Marty Allen), the kids would all laugh.

There were many segments that were seen at the start of the show, such as Bob going into the audience and asking the kids, "Who has a joke?"

With "Tongue Twisters", Bob asked them to say a funny name or city really fast, three times.

In the "Top Hat Ball Toss", a kid would put on a top hat and try to toss a ping pong ball on the top of it.

Other opening segments included a kid trying to whistle while they stuff crackers in their mouth. Bob would ask another kid if they were a good estimator and if they could guess how long a certain item was, or how much it weighed. Then he'd turn to another kid and say, "Name three things in your pocket."

"Cups and Saucers" was a test of skill that offered multiple prizes if a kid could balance saucers and cups on top of each other, while at the same time, trying to hold a bunch of toys under their arms and legs.

Even more segments at the beginning of the show included, "Show and Tell", where Bob would ask the audience if anyone brought a specific item from home ("Who has a rubber band?"). This later changed when Bob would ask if anyone had something unusual, like an aardvark. Bob would then sing, "Has Anyone Here Got An Aardvark?"

"What Do You Wanna Be When You Grow Up?" is what Bob would ask different kids in the audience and their responses were usually, "A fireman"...."a baseball player"...."an astronaut"...."a teacher."

In "Pass It On", Bob would whisper a secret into a kid's ear and then tell them to "pass it on" to the rest of the kids in that row. The last kid was then asked to repeat out loud what Bob's secret was and it was usually something very different than what Bob actually said.

"The Telephone Game" involved contestants calling up somebody and if that person on the other end of the line said a secret word before the buzzer sounded, a siren went off and the contestant won a prize.

The last of the show's early segments was, "What The Heck Is It?", in which Bob would hold up an obscure object (like an ugly fruit) and the audience would try to guess what it was. After they were stumped, a voice with a thick Yiddish accent would ask, "Vhat da heck izzit?" and Bob would give the answer.

The segments and games which followed were some of Wonderama's most popular, usually involving a larger audience participation.

"The Krazy Kar Race" - Three teams of kids would race to a certain mark, then turn around and race back to where a teammate would take over and do the same thing, with the winning team getting a prize.

The kids would do jumping jacks, push-ups, and four count burpees, then Bob would sing his famous song, "Exercise." When he yelled, "And Freeze!", the camera would zoom in on a few kids trying to stand still.

"Eye Spy" aka "Disguise Delimit" - A kid's photo was shown and then a group of five kids came out dressed in disguise, trying to convince a chosen member from the audience that they're the kid in the photo.

"Guess What I'm Doing!" - Bob (as Wally Wonderful), presided over various kids who would pantomime different things (i.e., Houdini in a straight jacket) and the audience would guess what they were doing.

"Bob's Bamboozlers" - Bob would gather a bunch of kids around him, perform a couple of neat magic tricks and then show them how he did it.

"Eye Witness" - A guest would come out wearing a kooky outfit and make-up and after talking to Bob, they'd leave and the kids would have to remember certain details about them if they wanted to win a prize.

"Guess Your Best" - Hosted by Bert Youtiful (Bob), where three contestants had to predict the outcome of various stunts. Each correct answer earned a point, and in the final round, contestants bet any or all of their points on a final stunt (similar to final Jeopardy). The winner would receive the grand prize, usually an Odyssey game.

"The Good News Room" - Three kids dressed as reporters with typewriters would read various news stories off a teleprompter.

"Apple On A String Game" - Three kids with their hands behind their back, attempt to take a bite out of an apple while it swung from a string.

"Hopscotch" - A kid was chosen from the audience to play hopscotch, and at the same time, try to pick up as many toys and games as they could without dropping them, then turn around and hop back to the starting point and whatever toys they held on to, they got to keep.

Bob as "Professor Fingleheimer" (with a German accent), would ask the kids in the audience goofy trivia questions, prompting them to blow on their kazoos in unison. Bob would press down on an old squeeze horn and then sing, "The Fingleheimer Song."

Usually right before a commercial, Bob would appear as the "Crazy Magician", with a black mustache and oracle's hat, waving his magic wand and performing a magic trick, which was shown in reverse.

"Snake Cans" was probably Wonderama's most popular game, mainly because the winner would take home all the games and toys on the studio floor, which included a new Ross Apollo bicycle with the banana seat.

Bob randomly picked 10 kids from the audience who had to choose one of 10 snake cans sitting in a row on a long table and then try to twist off the can's lid.

Most of the time, when a kid unscrewed the top of the can, a bunch of coiled snakes would pop in the air, as a "Boing!" sound effect went off. Bob would then ask each kid a question and if they answered correctly, they would get a toy.

When only a few snake cans were left standing, the kids went into a frenzy. They all wanted to be the one to twist off the lid and see the winning bouquet of flowers inside. After all, being the big winner on Wonderama was every child's dream and something they'd never forget.

Some of the prizes given away during Snake Cans included Headache, Tension, Stay Alive, Spirograph, Talking View Master, Toss Across, Tool Belt, The Six-Million Dollar Man action figure, a giant Tootsie Roll, an inflatable jar of Skippy Peanut Butter, and a Ross 3-speed bicycle.

When Bob asked, "Who's ready for Snake Cans?" All hands went up!

Bob would always go over all the prizes that were up for grabs.

With two snake cans left and no winner, the kids would go berserk!

You never knew who was going to the pick the right can and win it all.

"Wonderama Go-Go" (later "Disco City") - Kids danced on top of a three-foot box to the latest Top 40 hits in the Wonderama Go-Go cellar (actually just the other side of the studio) and the winner of the dance-off got a brand new Apollo 3 bike. "Crocodile Rock" and "You Build Me Up Buttercup" were played almost every week. The dance segments were always interrupted by "The Disco Kid", a young boy dressed as the Lone Ranger who would gallop into the studio and hand Bob a 7-inch single.

"Head's Up" - Musical chairs with hats, as Bob would put six black hats on six kids and they would have to remove them and put them on the kid next to them (forwards, and in reverse) until two kids were left, then Bob would speed it up until one of them was declared the winner.

"Paper Hop" - Three teams of three kids would hop from one side of the studio to the other on a large piece of paper. The team that finished first without tearing their paper was the winner.

"Pop The Balloon On The Mattress" - Three teams of two kids would try to sit on and burst as many balloons on a mattress that they could before time expired.

"Limbo" - Three teams of five kids had to join hands and crawl under a long pole, and every time they made it, the pole was lowered even more. Needless to say, the shortest and skinniest team usually won.

"Kids On The Block" - Bob would open a door, and one by one, half a dozen kids would emerge and depending on the topic, would recall a funny story about themselves or their parents.

There were many other segments and games as well, such as "You Bet Your Face" aka "The Whose Is Whose Is Whose" (with Bob as Chuck Roast). A kid from the audience tried to match a group of children with their real parents who were also sitting in a small group. The audience would either agree or disagree if the matches were correct. It was funny how some families looked alike and some did not.

"Make-Up", had kids putting on theatrical paint and powder in front of make-up mirrors while the song, "An Actor's Life For Me" was played in the background. The kids in the audience would vote for the best make-up job via the applause meter.

"Picture This" (with Bob as Art Art), where kids would draw on giant plexiglass sheets with oil-based pastel chalks while the song, "Love is Blue" was played in the background.

Another popular game was "Simon Sez", led by Lou Goldstein, who was a master at tricking the kids into doing things without him saying, "Simon Sez." The last kid standing who didn't fall for any of Goldstein's trickery would win a prize.

Rounding out the rest of Wonderama's segments and games was "Observation", as a group of kids were dressed alike. The audience had to take a good look at them before they were hidden behind a wall and Bob would ask questions about them.

"The Balloon Bottom Race" - Kids would run up to a cage filled with balloons, grab one, run back, sit on it and burst it. The kid who burst the most balloons won.

"Toss A Ball and Catch A Prize" - Kids would throw a ball in the air, pick up a toy, and catch the ball. If they caught it, they could keep the toy. Greedy kids always went for the big boxed toys like Toss Across and Ricochet and never could catch the ball.

"Marshmallows On Strings" - Accompanied by Bob's song, "Marshmallows Are Funny", kids would choose one of four long ropes to pull on, which were attached to an unseen scaffold. When the ropes were yanked on, rubber bricks or huge quantities of ping pong balls came down. If a kid happened to pull on the right rope, a new Raleigh bicycle came sliding down unto the studio floor with lots of confetti.

"The Ball and Blanket Game" - Teams of kids had to throw beach balls on to blankets held by their teammates who then passed it on to other kids holding blankets until it got to the end of the line. The team that got the most beach balls to the end after two minutes won.

"Pet Peeves" - Different kids stood before a camera for 20-seconds to rail about a pet peeve, like not being able to chew gum in school, or taking out the garbage. Each speech was punctuated by nine organ notes at the end (sort of a connotation of irritation).

Near the end of its run, Wonderama added a "Kid Interview" which Bob would conduct as the show was winding down, getting a kids perspective on life, family, friends, and school.

Three cast members were added in the show's final year, a decision that Bob was not happy about. "Shu Shu" the sarcastic lion, "Won Ton" the annoying robot, and "Max the Gypsy" a talking head, inside a box.

Bob would wrap up every show by giving everyone in the audience "Free Goodies" which included: Good Humor Ice Cream, RC Cola, Kraus Hot Dogs, Hostess Twinkies, Nandy Candy, No Jelly Candy Bars, Goo Goo Clusters, Georgia Peanuts, Lender's Bagelettes, Charms Blow Pops, Beach-Nut Fruit Stripe Gum, Goobers, Duncan Yo-Yo's, Silly Putty, Oral B toothbrushes, and Dynamite Magazine.

Every episode of Wonderama ended with Bob singing his signature song, "Kids Are People Too." As the closing credits rolled, the kids in the grandstand would slowly wave their hands and arms in the air.

During his years hosting Wonderama, Bob also made personal appearances across the country, meeting his young fans. Whether he was signing autographs, promoting his albums, or appearing on stage at "Live" Wonderama shows, Bob simply enjoyed talking to children.

CHAPTER 5

Learning New Things

Even though Bob had stated that Wonderama was more about
entertaining kids, as opposed to educating them, there were still segments
on the show that allowed for Bob and the kids in the audience to learn
new things, thanks to all the Wonderema guests who were experts in their
specific fields. In some cases, their particular segment introduced the
kids to something new, or something they had never experienced or seen
up close. For example, for the kids who had never gone bowling before,
a one-lane bowling alley with pins was set up in the studio where
professional bowler and instructor Don Johnson (above) taught Bob the
basics of how to grip a bowling ball and throw it down the lane. Just one
of many "How to" segments on Wonderama over the years.

Bob learning how to paint with art teacher Conni Gordon.

Bob learning how to walk in Medieval armor.

Bob learning how to race Hot Wheels.

Bob learning how to walk in a Deep Sea Diver suit.

Bob learning fitness exercises with instructor Suzy Prudden.

Bob learning how to hop on a Pogo Stick.

Bob learning the Heimlich maneuver with Dr. Henry Heimlich.

Bob learning competitive fencing.

Bob learning how Olympic swimmers dive into a pool.

Bob learning how to be a rodeo rider.

Bob learning how to jump on a trampoline.

Bob learning the art of mime with Marcel Marceau.

Bob learning to play the flute with Shirley Cothran, Miss America 1975.

Bob learning stunt work with Knott's Berry Farm Funfighters.

Bob singing opera with opera singers Richard Tucker and Robert Merrill.

Bob learning how to hang from a trapeze.

Bob learning how to tackle with NFL great Rosie Greer.

Bob learning how to bake a cake with Julie Nixon Eisenhower.

Bob learning how to tap dance with Donald O'Connor.

Bob learning how to tie-dye a T-shirt.

Bob wrestling with comedian Marty Allen.

Bob playing baseball with Johnny Bench and The Bad News Bears.

Bob learning to play tennis with Arthur Ashe.

Bob learning how to fight a bear.

Bob learning to shoot a basketball with NBA star Bill Bradley.

Bob learning to play chess with child prodigy Robert LeDonne.

CHAPTER 6

Guests & Performers

Wonderama was the most popular children's show on Sunday mornings not only because of Bob McAllister and his fun segments and games, but because of the top-notch guests and performers who would appear on the show, such as legendary voice actor Mel Blanc (above).

In 1970, after hosting the show for three years, Bob thought it would be great to start booking world-class entertainment that the kids would really love, which would include famous names from the world of film, television, music, sports, comedy, magic, and the arts. There aren't enough pages in this book to document every single guest that appeared on Wonderama, but many of them can be seen in this chapter.

Billy Crystal (Comedian).

Danny Bonaduce ("The Partridge Family").

Dick Gautier ("Get Smart").

Dick Van Dyke ("The Dick Van Dyke Show").

Fred Travalena (Celebrity Impressionist).

Gary Burghoff ("M*A*S*H").

Jerry Lewis (Actor/Director/Host of the MDA Telethon).

Henry Gibson ("Laugh-In").

Jim Backus ("Mr. Magoo") trying to guess the food that he's touching.

Jo Anne Worley ("Laugh-In").

Johnny Whitaker ("Sigmund and the Sea Monsters").

Karen Valentine ("Room 222").

Marlo Thomas ("That Girl").

Paul Lynde ("The Hollywood Squares").

Phyllis Diller (Actress/Comedian).

Penny Marshall and Cindy Williams ("Laverne & Shirley").

Telly Savalas ("Kojak").

Terry Jones and Michael Palin ("Monty Python's Flying Circus").

Ben Vereen (Actor/Dancer/Singer).

Bobby Van (Actor/Dancer).

Cyril Ritchard (Captain Hook in "Peter Pan").

The Hudson Brothers ("The Hudson Brothers Razzle Dazzle Show").

Jim Henson (Puppeteer and Creator of "The Muppets").

Rod McKuen (Poet/Singer/Songwriter).

Rodney Dangerfield (Comedian).

Soupy Sales (Children's Television Host).

Steve Allen (Writer/Composer/Comedian).

Bob Clampett (Animator and Creator of "Beany and Cecil").

Bob Keeshan ("Captain Kangaroo").

Colonel Harland Sanders (Founder of Kentucky Fried Chicken).

Jacques Cousteau (Oceanographer/Filmmaker).

LeRoy Neiman (Expressionist Painter).

Stan Lee (Comic Book Icon).

Wolfman Jack (Radio Personality).

George Barris (Custom Car Designer and Builder).

Sonny Fox, the previous host of Wonderama, visiting Bob backstage.

Billie Jean King (Women's Tennis Champion).

Dave DeBusschere (NBA Basketball Star).

Dwight Stones (Olympic High Jump Record Setter).

Earl "The Pearl" Monroe (NBA Basketball Star).

Evel Knievel (Daredevil).

Joe Garagiola (Major League Baseball Broadcaster).

Reggie Jackson (Major League Baseball Star).

Gene Michael (Major League Baseball Shortstop).

Tracy Austin (Tennis Player).

Norm Snead (NFL Quarterback).

Walt "Clyde" Frazier (NBA Basketball Star).

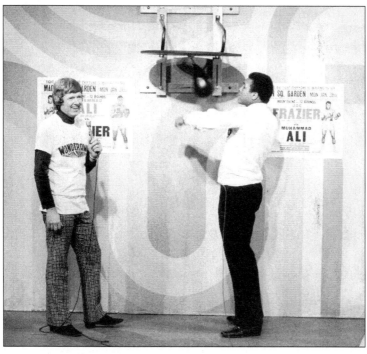

Muhammad Ali (Heavyweight Boxing Champion).

Joe Frazier (Heavyweight Boxing Champion).

Ali vs. Frazier in a game of marbles before their big heavyweight fight.

Since Bob McAllister was a magician himself, it was no surprise that magic was a big part of Wonderama, as the world's greatest magicians all appeared on the show. In fact, Bob had more magician's perform on Wonderama than any other show on television. They included Slydini, Alan Shaxon, Tony Spina, Al Delage, Shimada, Milbourne Christopher, Duke Stern, Michael Bailey, Milbourne Richiardi, David Copperfield, Al Flosso (above), Harry Blackstone Jr. (below), and many others.

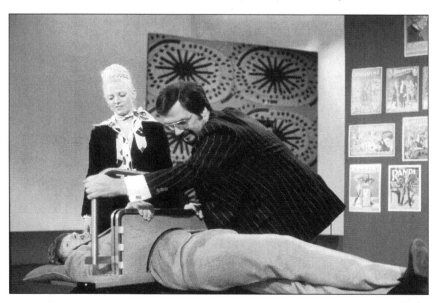

Doug Henning.

Carl Ballentine.

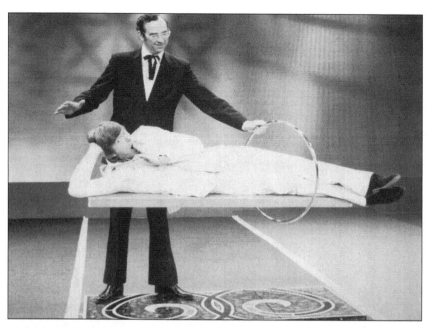

Walter Zaney Blaney.

Mark Wilson.

Ali Bongo.

Peter Pit.

Singers, songwriters, solo musicians, and bands from all genres (rock, pop, jazz, blues, R&B, and Broadway) appeared on Wonderama almost every week to either promote a new album, or an upcoming tour. The show featured a wide range of musical guests that the kids in the audience could enjoy in-person. From pop bands like ABBA (above) to the cast of the Broadway show, "Annie" (below), plus many others.

Billy Preston.

The Bay City Rollers.

David Essex.

Burt Bacharach.

Donovan.

Don McLean.

Eubie Blake.

The Fifth Dimension.

Harry Chapin.

Gladys Knight and the Pips.

José Feliciano.

Lionel Hampton.

Marvin Hamlisch.

Neil Sedaka.

Pearl Bailey.

Richard Rodgers.

Richie Havens.

Roger Daltrey.

Stevie Wonder.

The Jacksons.

The Miracles.

The Supremes.

CHAPTER 7

Songs & Albums

A big part of Wonderama's appeal and charm were the catchy songs that Bob would sing to the kids during the course of the show. Even today, a lot of us can still sing along to those wonderful songs, such as "Exercise" and "Kids Are People Too." Not only were these songs sung on the show, but they appeared on three Wonderama-related albums that Bob put out, which were all fun and family friendly. The first of these albums, "Bob McAllister of Wonderama" (1969), was co-written and composed with Joe Raposo of Sesame Street fame. The second and third albums, "Kids Are People Too" (1971), and "Oh Gee, It's Great To Be A Kid" (1975), were co-written and arranged with Artie Kaplan.

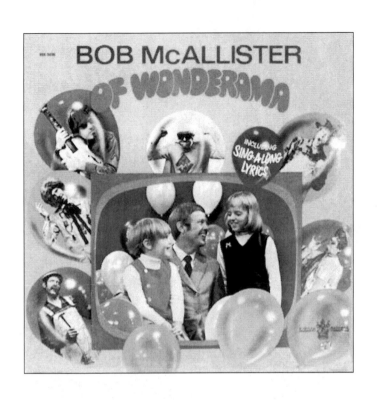

From the three albums, there were seven songs that were sung on Wonderama the most. "Mike Fury Is A Goody" (from 1967-70 only), "Hello, Hello" "Good News", "Aardvark", "Fingleheimer" "Exercise", and "Kids Are People Too". An eighth song, "I'm Somebody", was sung on the final show in 1977 with Bob's youngest daughter, Molly Jo.

On three different occasions, somebody other than Bob sang "Kids Are People Too" on Wonderama. Ralph Carter (Michael on "Good Times") joined Bob in a duet; Opera singer Roberta Peters and stage actor Cyril Ritchard joined Bob in another rendition, as Ritchard, on cue, would look at the camera and say, "Wackadoo, wackadoo, wackadoo"; Florida kiddie show host "Skipper" Chuck Zink led a chorus of youngsters in yet another version of the song.

Also worth mentioning are the memorable pieces of incidental music that played in the background during certain Wonderama segments and games, like "I Ain't Down Yet" (Meredith Wilson), "Java" (Al Hirt), "They're Off" (Henry Mancini), "Baby Elephant Walk" (Henry Mancini), "Everything's Coming Up Roses" (Jule Styne), "Bathtub Saturday Night" (Neal Hefti), "Yakety Sax" (Boots Randolph), "An Actor's Life For Me" (Leigh Herline), and "Whipped Cream" (Pete Fountain).

HELLO, HELLO

Hello, hello
Hello, hello
How are you today?...Fine
Gee it's good to see you ya
And that's why I'm here to say

Hello, hello
Hello, hello
We can have some fun
There's songs to sing and games to play
Something for everyone

Now turn to your neighbor and say hello
One, two, three...Hello
Turn to the other and say how do
One, two, three...How do
Turn to the person in back and say
It's a great, great day, Everybody

Hello, hello
Hello, hello
Every girl and boy
If you're really with it
Let me hear you shout for joy...Yeah!

Hello, hello
Hello, hello
Everybody call your name
Gee it's good to see ya
Hey I'm really glad you came

GOOD NEWS

Oh have you heard any good news today, today
I wanna hear what you have to say
Wait till I get to the count of three
And tell me all the good news you have for me
One, two, three
Well now that's really good news
I'm happy to say
Good good news today

EXERCISE

Exercise, exercise
Come on everybody do your exercise
Exercise, exercise
Come on everybody do your exercise

Jumpin' jack, jumpin' jack
Come on everybody do the jumpin' jack
Jumpin' jack, jumpin' jack
Come on everybody do the jumpin' jack
And freeze

Hands on hips, hands on hips
Touch your toes with your fingertips
Hands on hips, hands on hips
Touch your toes with your fingertips
And freeze

Stand up straight, shake 'em out
Let me see you twist your body all about
Stand up straight, shake 'em out
Let me see you twist your body all about
And freeze

FINGLEHEIMER

Fingleheimer
Fingleheimer
Fingle Dingle Heimer
Fingleheimer
Fingleheimer
Fingle Dingle Heimer
The more you Fingle
The less you Heimer
The less you Heimer
The more you Fingle
Fingleheimer
Fingleheimer
Fingle Dingle Heimer

KIDS ARE PEOPLE TOO

We may be young and not full grown
But we have problems of our own
Kids are people too

And though we're small, we do our best
To do our thing just like the rest
Kids are people too

It isn't easy going all day
Winning and losing in the games that we play
Doing our homework, learning in school
And trying to live by the golden rule

And so we hope you'll understand
And try to lend a helping hand
Kids are people too

HAS ANYONE HERE GOT AN AARDVARK?

Has anybody here got an aardvark?
Has anybody here got an aardvark?
Everyone here has a right and left ear
But nobody here has an aardvark

You're a dandy group, there's a can of soup
There's a hula hoop and a kid with a toupe
Everything's cute but it doesn't really suit
Cause nobody here's got an aardvark

Has anybody here got an aardvark?
Has anybody here got an aardvark?
Everyone here has a right and left ear
But nobody here has an aardvark

There's a girl over there with a grizzly bear
There's a girl over there with a ribbon in her hair
There's a girl in a chair with her finger in the air
But nobody here has an aardvark

Has anybody here got an aardvark?
Has anybody here got an aardvark?
Everyone here has a right and left ear
But nobody here has an aardvark

There's a boy named Roy and he's holding a toy
There's a boy named Troy and he's jumping for joy
There's a boy kinda coy cause he hasn't won a toy
Cause nobody here has an aardvark

MIKE FURY IS A GOODY

Mike Fury is a goody
Mike Fury is a goody
I brush my super teeth
I wash my super feet
I blow my super nose...Why?
Cause I'm a goody
He's a goody
Mike Fury is a goody
I wear a super belt...Why?
Cause it holds my super pants up
And I'm a goody
He's a goody
Mike Fury is a goody
I never bite my super nails...Why?
Cause it makes my super feet sore
And I'm a goody
He's a goody
Mike Fury is a goody
I always eat a super onion...Why?
Cause it makes me super strong
And I'm a goody
He's a goody
Mike Fury is a goody
I always keep my super chin up...Why?
Cause it keeps milk from spilling on my super clothes
And I'm a goody
He's a goody
Mike Fury is a goody
I always drink my super milk...Why?
Cause it gives the super cows something to do
And I'm a goody
He's a goody
Mike Fury is a goody
Mike Fury is a goody

CHAPTER 8

The End of an Era

In 1977, Wonderama's 22nd season and Bob McAllister's 10th as host, a sign that something wasn't quite right began with the very first show when Bob introduced three new cast members that took all of Wonderama's fans by surprise, not to mention, Bob himself. A wise-cracking lion, a loud annoying robot, and a talking head, were all added to the show. These three characters simply did not blend well with Bob's usual interaction with the kids. They were all obnoxious and would always interrupt Bob throughout the show with their humorless antics. Privately, Bob made it known that he didn't like these new characters, but not wanting to rock the boat, Bob hesitantly went along with it.

To make matters worse, Wonderama was suddenly shortened from three hours to two hours and pushed back to 7 a.m., instead of its normal 8 a.m. to 11 a.m. time slot on Sunday morning. Even the wait for tickets was changed. Instead of first-come, first-served, the system became a lottery, tossing all the kids' names into a large hat and the winners would be picked from that.

During the 1977 season, Wonderama was on every Sunday with its usual games, contests, songs, and segments, but on November 21st, a shocking announcement was made by WNEW-TV's general manager, James Coppersmith. Wonderama was being cancelled after nearly a quarter of a century of being on the air, with it's December 25th Christmas show being the last episode. This was despite Wonderama's extremely high ratings on Sunday, where it captivated 60% of all TV sets in New York and a 90% share in Washington. Coppersmith denied reports that it was a budget-cutting decision, stating that after 22 years it was time for a change. Bob, Art Stark (producer), and all of Bob's staff were given pink slips. Bob's first reaction was, "I feel terrible, hurt, and angry. I guess it's cheaper and easier for the station to run cartoons, despite the fact we have a large audience and loyal following."

The final Wonderama episode was a somber one. Yes, all the familiar games and contests were played, but on this special occasion, about 25 celebrities appeared on the show (waving their AFTRA scale of $325.00) to pay their respects to Bob and say farewell, such as Harry Chapin, Jo Anne Worley, Stan Lee, and Soupy Sales, who read consolation telegrams from many other celebrities who couldn't attend. Many staff members were in tears throughout the whole taping. After singing a touching duet of "I'm Somebody" with his three-year-old daughter Molly Jo (above), Bob ended the last Wonderama show by thanking his staff and everyone at home for watching, and even Metromedia. A slight quiver surfaced in his voice as he signed off. "Choose what you watch on television carefully and be sure and read books." Bob then said goodbye, sang "Kids Are People Too" and walked off the set for the very last time to a loud applause. After the final show was broadcast, Metromedia began airing re-runs of Wonderama for the next two years with the celebrity guests and musical performances edited out, since the station didn't want to pay the royalty fees.

The reality was that Wonderama's cancellation was just part of a trend in children's television at the time. Programs with live entertainment were being phased out and cartoon reruns were being used as replacements. The operative strategy of many station managers was, "Who needs production staffs, salaries, benefits, and all the hassle?"

In 1978, Bob wrote an open letter in Variety magazine voicing his disappointment that Metromedia had edited out all guests from the Wonderama re-runs and that children were missing out on seeing quality television. He went on to write how devastated he was to learn that most of Wonderama's tapes were destroyed or bulk erased (which they were).

Just when things couldn't get any worse, Bob wrote another open letter regarding Wonderama in 1980, this time in the New York Times and it was startling. It began with, "Do not allow your children to watch Wonderama. It is surrounded by violence." Bob was referring to a commercial for the violent Charles Bronson film, "The Mechanic", which ran several times throughout a Wonderama re-run and featured a man with a sawed-off shotgun shooting and killing several people. Bob went on to say that he could longer recommend Wonderama as a quality product. WNEW-TV's vice-president Muriel Reis responded that it was simply an inadvertent computer error, which Bob did not believe for one second. These incidents reinforced Bob's commitment in speaking out against TV violence and becoming a champion for quality children's programming, right up until the day he died.

CHAPTER 9

Bob, After Wonderama

Less than a year after Wonderama's cancellation, Bob's career received a needed boost when in September 1978, he started hosting a new ABC network children's show called, "Kids Are People Too", which aired Sunday mornings from 10 a.m. to 11:30 a.m. and was taped in front of a live studio audience (ages 10 to 15) at the Elysee Theatre on West 58th Street in New York.

Bob was very exited about this new venture which he was led to believe would be very similar to Wonderama, but after the show's first taping, there was friction between Bob and ABC.

Bob was disappointed that he couldn't sing his trademark songs and none of Wonderama's games or contests would be added either. It was mostly a celebrity interview show with reruns of "Wonderbug" and "Super Friends" thrown in for good measure, but what irked Bob the most was that the network wanted him to read from cue cards, which would negate any spontaneity or ad-libbing which Bob was used to. However, Bob really wanted the show to work, so he swallowed his pride and went forward with the network's demands.

ABC promoted "Kids Are People Too" very heavily and Bob hosted the show's first 11 episodes very professionally. Things seems to be going smoothly enough, as Bob interviewed a variety of guests, such as actor/singer Joel Grey, NBA star Julius Erving, Disney animator Ward Kimball, and consumer advocate Ralph Nader, when suddenly Bob was unceremoniously fired and was later replaced by a much younger and less experienced host named Michael Young.

Squire Rushnell, ABC's vice-president of children's programming said there were several problems with Bob as host. Aside from Bob having trouble with the cue cards, his segments with a talking dog named "Wack A Doo" wasn't going over well. Neither was Bob's new gimmick of bouncing a rubber ball on stage while he talked to the kids. Last but not least, "Kids Are People Too" was designed to attract an older children's audience and Bob was more comfortable with younger children. In all, it just wasn't working out as the network had planned.

Bob saw his dealings with the network much differently. The freedom he was promised when he signed up to host "Kids Are People Too" never transpired. Instead, Bob saw himself as a puppet being forced to read cue cards and was only permitted minimal contact with the audience and guests. He disagreed with the show's content, the handling of the children, and the handling of the guests. On top of that, he was upset with the show's editing, as portions of his interviews were cut to make room for cartoons. Bob was embarrassed having to say to Ralph Nader or pianist Victor Borge, "It's been nice talking to you but right now it's time for Super Friends."

Even though Bob was no longer the host of "Kids Are People Too", he did, in fact, own the show's title and format, so he licensed them both to ABC for five years, making himself a pretty penny.

Not one to rest on his laurels, Bob moved on from the "Kids Are People Too" fiasco and kept busy over the next two decades with many new and exciting projects that he would immerse himself in.

In 1983, Bob stayed in Los Angeles, California for two weeks and did a week's worth of magic shows at the Magic Castle for packed houses every night. Bob was performing in front of the likes of Cary Grant (above), David Niven, and many other celebrities who all loved Bob's magic shows. Castle owner Milt Larson couldn't have been happier for Bob.

Bob briefly returned to children's television in 1986 when he appeared on the 10-part PBS Series, "Tuned In", where he played a junior high school teacher who tries to get his students to monitor their TV viewing by creating and hosting their own TV news show.

For the remainder of his life, Bob performed magic at corporate banquets, picnics, comedy clubs, and amusement parks. He also taught magic at adult classes at Stuyvesant High School in New York City and performed regularly at the Mostly Magic Club in Greenwich Village.

Bob found the time to invent new tricks and produce instructional videos on magic. He was honored by the Society of American Magicians and the International Brotherhood of Magicians for his lifelong work in the field of magic.

An avid roller skater since the late 1970s, Bob opened "The People Palace" (above), a short-lived, outdoor skating rink that Bob invested a lot of money in.

Throughout the 1990s, Bob could still be seen roller skating all over Manhattan. Even when he was very ill, Bob made the rounds of Manhattan magic supply shops, while on roller skates.

His last public appearance was at an IKEA store in New Jersey in 1997 where he and Bob Keeshan ("Captain Kangaroo") introduced a line of kids furniture.

On July 21, 1998, Bob eventually succumbed to lung cancer at the age of 63.

BOB McALLISTER

Bob was twice married, twice divorced, and the father of three girls: Susan, Robin, and Molly Jo. Ironically, Bob died the same week as two other legendary hosts of children's shows, Buffalo Bob Smith and Shari Lewis.

Shortly before his death in 1998, Bob had talked enthusiastically about doing a children's show again. Sadly, that show was never produced.

What's even more sad is that outside of some short clips on YouTube and a couple of poorly made VHS bootlegs that are around, none of Wonderama's original tapes were preserved or saved. It is indeed a "lost" show, but hopefully after reading this book, the memories of Bob McAllister and Wonderama will stay with you, and that one day, you can pass on those memories to your children, and perhaps they will pass it on to theirs.